You're PAWSOME Bailey Buckets!

How an adopted dog helps a boy discover The meaning of FRIENDSHIP.

By Kris Szabo
Ridge View Publishers
Illustrated by Illustrative Agency

Copyright

Dedication

To Jack, Ila, and Dan: Thank you for your love, support, and patience. And to Bailey, for all the love, licks, and muddy paw prints.

Jake was a lonely boy who spent much of his time playing video games or watching tv. Whenever his parents asked him how school was, Jake would quietly reply, "Fine."

"I'm worried about him." Jake heard his mom whisper to his dad. Jake's heart sank and he just stared at the tv.

"Come here, Jake. We have something we want to talk to you about," said his father. Jake was worried this was going to be another one of those talks.

His parents were concerned about him and hopeful that a puppy would change that. They told Jake that on Saturday they would go to the pound and look for a puppy. Jake didn't say anything and doubted he'd find one he liked. Just something else to annoy him, he thought.

On Saturday, they left the house early to get to the dog pound. They were the first ones in line to select a puppy. Today was the big day for the puppies and the pound was filled with energetic pups trying to get everyone's attention.

Bailey was so excited. It was adoption day.
Today she gets to pick her human!

As soon as Bailey saw Jake, her tail
started to wag and she began to
whimper. "He's the one!" she thought.
She knew it with all her heart. She
kept looking at Jake hoping he would
come to her crate. But he didn't
seem to notice her at all.

There were so many puppies to choose from. Jake looked around for a bit. He wasn't sure how he would ever be able to choose one. He went from crate to crate inspecting each puppy.

That one was too barky. And that one was too shaggy. And that one was too drooly. And that one was too jumpy. Not a single puppy caught his eye.

Then he saw her. A small white puppy with brown spots and ears that went in two directions. One ear was up straight and the other flopped to the side. She had a small tag with her name printed on it. Bailey.

Bailey grew more excited as Jake came closer to
her crate. When Jake knelt down Bailey leaned in
and licked his face. Her tail wagged so fast it was
making a snapping sound in the crate.
Jake laughed and gave her a pat on
the head.

Jake smiled and shouted,
"This one! This is the one I want."
Bailey was certain they would be
best friends.

When they got home, Jake
happily showed Bailey where
her water bowl, food bowl,
and bed were located.
It was the first time Jake's
parents had seen him happy in
a long time.

Bailey was thrilled to be part of this new family. She followed Jake everywhere!

Every morning, Bailey jumped on Jake's bed to wake him and to start their day together.

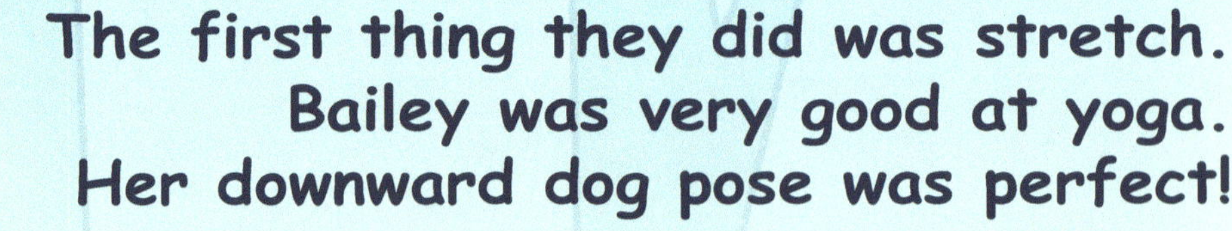

The first thing they did was stretch.
Bailey was very good at yoga.
Her downward dog pose was perfect!

Everyday, when Jake got home from
school they would go for long walks.
Along the way they stopped to look
at the flowers and the trees.

Jake often noticed something new or beautiful and would point it out to Bailey. She loved listening to him. Bailey was learning a lot about the world from Jake. He was a smart boy.

Sometimes, they ran around and played ball until they were tired or hungry. Jake loved playing outside with Bailey. She was really good at catching. Jake was having so much fun he didn't even miss watching tv or playing video games.

Jake even taught Bailey how to hug and high five. Every time they did this he said, "You're Pawsome, Bailey Buckets!"

Jake's parents were pleased to see Jake smiling, laughing, and spending time outside. And most of all for having found a best friend.

Some days Jake and Bailey sat quietly in the grass and stared up at the clouds in the sky. They loved using their imaginations. Bailey always saw squirrel and bone shapes, which made her happy.

They would go on adventures and explore the backyard. They often found little critters and moved them to safe places.

Jake would say, "It's important to take care of all creatures, big and small." Bailey wagged her tail in agreement. Bailey always jumped when a toad or frog would spring up in the grass.

"You're okay, girl. It's just a frog," Jake would say laughing and patting her head. It was so funny to see her jump from something so tiny.

Bailey was a good listener and loved hearing all about Jake's day or listening to him read. She even helped him with his homework. Mostly, she just listened but sometimes she encouraged him to take a break and play or get a snack.

This helped Jake's confidence and he began sharing his thoughts and feelings with her, too.

Bailey was good at keeping secrets. And Jake was great at telling jokes. Jake's parents were overjoyed to see and hear him happy.

Rainy days were the best! Jake would get his boots and raincoat and run outside with Bailey. "No rain is going to stop us," he shouted as they ran out the door. They would jump in the puddles. Bailey splashed and barked.
Jake laughed and yelled "Mud Puppy!" They were such a mess!

Bailey was also a good snuggler. She would keep Jake company and cuddle when Jake wasn't feeling well. She even shared her toys with him. Sometimes Bailey would bury her cookies under his pillow for safe keeping. Jake always giggled when he found a biscuit under his pillow.

The best days were when they just sat, side by side, and said nothing. Bailey liked that the most. She could tell how much Jake loved her and she felt like the luckiest dog in the world. Bailey loved having a friend and so did Jake.

"Bailey, the best friends are the ones who
know what you're feeling without saying a
word and love you for who you truly are,"
said Jake as he patted her on the head.
Bailey licked Jake's cheek and leaned into his
shoulder and they both sighed.